Managing Your
M☉ney

Kristy Stark, M.A.Ed.

Consultant

Chrissy Johnson, M.Ed.
Elementary School Teacher
Cedar Point Elementary

Publishing Credits

Rachelle Cracchiolo, M.S.Ed., *Publisher*
Aubrie Nielsen, M.S.Ed., *EVP of Content Development*
Emily R. Smith, M.A.Ed., *VP of Content Development*
Véronique Bos, *Creative Director*
Robin Erickson, *Art Director*
Michelle Jovin, M.A., *Associate Editor*
Lee Aucoin, *Senior Graphic Designer*

Image Credits: p.17 Everett Historical; pg. 27 courtesy Lee Aucoin; all other images from iStock and/or Shutterstock.

Library of Congress Cataloging-in-Publication Data

Names: Stark, Kristy, author.
Title: Managing your money / Kristy Stark, M.A.Ed.
Description: Huntington Beach, CA : Teacher Created Materials, [2020] |
    Includes index. | Audience: Grades 2-3 | Summary: "Money plays a big
    role in everyone's life. Whether you have a little or a lot of money,
    people use it to buy the things they need and want. but, using money
    wisely takes careful planning and tracking. Explore ways to plan for
    your money, as well as earn more of it!"-- Provided by publisher.
Identifiers: LCCN 2020001597 (print) | LCCN 2020001598 (ebook) | ISBN
    9781087603872 (paperback) | ISBN 9781087603889 (ebook)
Subjects: LCSH: Money--Juvenile literature.
Classification: LCC HG221.5 .S75 2020 (print) | LCC HG221.5 (ebook) | DDC
    332.024--dc23
LC record available at https://lccn.loc.gov/2020001597
LC ebook record available at https://lccn.loc.gov/2020001598

**Teacher
Created
Materials**

5482 Argosy Avenue
Huntington Beach, CA 92649
www.tcmpub.com
ISBN 978-1-0876-0387-2
© 2020 Teacher Created Materials, Inc.
Printed in China 51497

Table of Contents

The Purpose of Money

Around the world, money comes in many different shapes, sizes, and colors. Some money has pictures of important people on it. Other types of money include symbols. These images represent the countries that make the money.

One thing is true about all types of money. Money has **value**. This means money can be used to pay for goods and services. Goods are things that people can buy, such as clothes or books. Services are things people pay other people to do for them. For example, people can pay someone to cook for them. People can use money to pay for goods and services.

Where Does It Come From?

Governments print their own money. In the United States, the Bureau of Engraving and Printing is in charge of printing paper money. All paper money printed in the United States is made at just two locations. The U.S. Mint makes coins. There are six of these locations around the country.

Counterfeit Money

Some people make fake money that is meant to look like real money. This is called **counterfeiting**. It is against the law. In the United States, paper money has special colors. It has hidden images too. Paper money is also printed on paper that only the government has. These special features make counterfeiting money more difficult.

Financial Goals

People set goals for their money. For instance, you might want to buy a new skateboard. Or you might set a goal to buy a gift for your mom's birthday. Adults often have more expensive goals than you have. They may want to buy a car or need to pay rent. People have lots of different **financial** goals. But they plan to meet those goals in similar ways.

Needs vs. Wants

There are things people need to live, such as clothes and food. There are also things that people want, such as toys and games. But wants are not things that people need in order to survive. People must learn to balance things that they really need with things that they want.

How Much Do You Need?

After you have a goal in mind, the first step is to find out how much money you will need. One way to do this is to research the price of the item you want. You can get an idea of the price by searching online. Or you can find the item in a store and check the price. Knowing how much something costs will help you make your plan.

Needs | Wants
food | candy
water | skateboard
clothes | video game

Walkie Talkies

$15.00

Average Cost of Food

One of the main needs people have is food. Food is also expensive. In 2019, U.S. households spent an average of $7,000 on food. That is more than $600 per month! People cannot live without food. So even though it can be expensive, they have to plan for it.

Managing Your Money

Once you have an idea of how much money you need to meet your goal, you should create a **budget**. A budget is a plan. It helps you balance your spending and saving. It is easier to make smart choices about what to do with your money when you have a budget.

Budgets can be **intimidating**. But they do not have to be difficult. Imagine you get $20 for doing yard work. You want to buy a birthday gift for a friend, but you also want to save for a new video game. So you create a budget. You plan to spend $10 on the gift. That means you will have $10 left to save for the game. With a plan in place, you can stay on track with your goals. This type of planning will help you **manage** your money.

Totaling Up

Part of a budget is called the "running total." Each time you spend money, you should subtract it from your running total. The money that is left is the amount you have left to save or spend.

BUDGET

yard work	$20
buy gift	-$10
running total	$10

Sales Tax

In many places, **sales tax** is added to the cost of an item. In the United States, the amount of sales tax depends on where the item is bought. Some states charge a higher sales tax than others. Five states do not charge any sales tax.

```
                 Receipt
    Adress: 1234 Lore
    Tel: 555-877-9248
    -------------------------------
    Date: 01-01              10:35
    -------------------------------
       toy                     6.50
       bracelet                7.50
       video games (2)        48.00
       watch                   9.30
       book                   11.90
       soda                    1.20
       gum                     0.40
    -------------------------------
    Sub-total                 84.80
    Sales Tax                  6.75
    Total                     91.15
```

Money Choices

It takes time to save money for a big purchase. It takes **patience** too. But you need to follow your budget to reach your goals. If not, you may end up spending money that you need. That is the hardest part of following a budget. You have to stick to your savings goals instead of spending money in the moment.

Imagine that you want to buy new shoes. The shoes cost $60. You receive $20 for your birthday. That means you still need to save $40 to buy the shoes. (The cost of the shoes minus the amount you received for your birthday equals the amount you still need to meet your goal.)

You still have a long way to go. But you will reach your goal faster if you stick to your budget and control how much you spend.

Budgeting Apps

There are many smartphone and tablet apps that can help people budget and keep track of their money. Some apps connect to **bank accounts**. These apps track all money going into and out of the accounts. The apps can also send alerts when people go over budget.

Saving Money

Your budget will tell you how much money you can spend and how much you should save. The next step is to think about where you will keep your money. You should put it in a safe place. You may want to save small amounts in a piggy bank or wallet. If you want to save a large amount of money, you may want to store it at a bank. An adult can help you open a bank account. A bank is a safe place to keep your money until you are ready to spend it.

Most adults use bank accounts to store their money. They may have both savings and checking accounts. Savings accounts help people save money. Checking accounts are used for spending. Most checking accounts also offer **debit cards** or checks to make spending easier. A check is a note that promises you will pay an amount of money.

The card front has the owner's name and account number.

Debit Card vs. Credit Card

A debit card is linked to a bank account. When the card is used, the money is instantly taken out of the account to pay for the purchase. A credit card works differently. When it is used, the credit card account is charged. Then, about a month later, the charge is listed on a credit card bill. The money does not come out of the person's bank account until they pay their bill.

Making Money

About six-tenths of American adults have jobs. They work to earn paychecks. They use that money to buy or rent things they need and want. Some people work more than one job. They may need a few jobs to make enough money to pay for their **expenses**.

Some jobs pay workers hourly wages. This means people get paid for each hour they work. These workers earn more money

Hourly Wage Example

Imagine you get paid $15 per hour. If you work 8 hours each day, you earn $120 per day.

$$\$15 \times 8 = \$120$$

hourly wage × hours worked = total amount earned per day of work

if they work more hours. They earn less money if they work fewer hours.

Some jobs pay workers a salary. This is a set amount of money paid over the course of a year. People who earn a salary earn the same amount in every paycheck. The salary is paid in equal amounts every month or every two weeks.

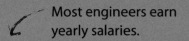
Most engineers earn yearly salaries.

Salary Example

Imagine you have a salary of $31,200 per year. That money is paid in equal amounts over the year. So you earn $2,600 per month.

$$\$31,200 \div 12 = \$2,600$$

yearly salary ÷ 12 months in a year = total amount earned per month of work

Jobs for Young People

Young people have wants and needs just like adults do. In the United States, though, children can't have jobs. There are laws that stop young people from working before they turn a certain age. Those laws change from state to state.

Even without jobs, young people can still find ways to earn money. Some young people start their own businesses. They do jobs based on things they are good at or love to do. For example, if you love dogs and being outdoors, you might start a business walking dogs for your neighbors. You can get paid for providing that service.

Children work in a factory in 1910.

Child Labor Laws

Children used to work long hours at dangerous jobs. These jobs kept children from going to school. Today, laws are in place to help working teenagers. These laws make sure that young workers are safe and limit how many hours they can work. These laws also stop students from working during the hours they should be in school.

Most jobs young people do are called service jobs. That is because they provide services for people. Doing yard work is a service young people can offer. Washing cars is a service too.

Young people can get creative when they work. In addition to service jobs, young people can make and sell goods. For example, if you like to make friendship bracelets, you can sell your jewelry at craft fairs or online.

No matter what job you do, you need to know how much to charge for your work. For instance, people may not want to pay $20 to have you wash their car. But you do not want to charge too little either. It can be hard work to wash a car. So, it would not make sense to be paid only $2 per car. Finding the right balance will help you succeed.

Electric Bill

ACCOUNT BALANCE
Previous Balance
Payment Received
Current Charges

Amount

SUMMARY OF CURRENT CHARGES
DELIVERY
SERVICES

Electric Service
Other Charges/Adjustments   34.44
Total Current Charges $3

ELECTRIC USAGE HISTORY (kWh)
700
560
420
280
140
0
M A M J J A S O N D J F M

Actual   ☐ Estimated

PLEASE PAY BY   AMOUNT D

Income and Expenses

A person's *income* is the amount of money they earn. This money can be earned many ways. For example, you might earn money for chores or get cash gifts on your birthday. *Expenses* are costs, or money spent. Most adults have monthly expenses, such as rent, the cost of groceries, and cell phone bills. People need to budget their spending so they are able to pay for these expenses. They should also try to save as much money as possible.

The goal of a business is to make money. But business owners must spend money too. They have to pay for their expenses. If you make bracelets, you need to buy beads and string. If you wash cars, you need to buy soap and sponges. These are called *planned expenses*. Other expenses are unplanned. When a tool breaks and you have to replace it, that is an *unplanned expense*. Unplanned expenses can cause a lot of stress for business owners.

Smart Spenders

When buying supplies for a business, it pays to do research. You may be able to find supplies cheaper. Or you may want to buy supplies in **bulk**. You will likely pay more in the beginning, but you will not have to buy supplies as often. Over time, that will help you save money.

The money left after all expenses are paid is called *profit*. You can save your profits. That will make unplanned expenses less stressful. Or you can spend your profits. You may want to use your profits to pay monthly expenses. Or you may want to spend money to grow your business. Your aim should be to find a good balance between spending and saving money.

Money Loss

Businesses lose money when they have more expenses than income. It is up to the owners to find solutions. The owners may find ways to lower expenses. Or they may have to raise prices to increase their profits.

A Plan in Action

This is Marie. She wants to buy a new glove before the softball season begins. Marie makes a plan to meet her goal. First, she researches which glove she wants and how much it will cost. She learns that the glove will cost $45 with sales tax. Now, she has a financial goal to work toward.

She thinks about what she likes to do and how to make it into a job. Since she already walks her dog every day, she decides that she could start a dog-walking service in her neighborhood. She thinks that customers would be willing to pay $5 per week. Marie decides this is a fair price.

Marie's Math

$$\$5 \times 3 = \$15$$

price per week ×
number of customers =
total money earned per week

Marie posts flyers in her neighborhood and gets three customers. So, her weekly income will be $15.

DOG
walker

Too busy?
Let Marie walk your dog!
$5 per week for 30 minutes of walking
on Mondays, Wednesdays, and Fridays

Call Marie
555-546-7980

Call Marie
555-546-7980

Call Marie
555-546-7980

Call Marie
555-546-7980

Call Marie
555-546-7980

Call Marie
555-546-7980

Watch It Grow!

There are ways to earn money without much effort. Money in a bank account can earn interest. That is money that banks reward people with when they keep money in their accounts. People can also **invest** in businesses. These people earn money when the businesses do well. Over time, people can make lots of money this way.

Marie now has an idea of how much income she will make. Her next step is to make a list of expenses for her business. She decides to buy dog treats. The treats will cost her $3 every other week. She needs to buy waste bags too. Marie will need to spend $5 each month on waste bags. She will pay for her expenses out of her weekly income.

Marie makes a spreadsheet to keep track of money she earns, spends, and saves. Unless her income or expenses change, Marie can expect to save $49 every four weeks. It will take her about a month to save enough to buy her softball glove.

	Week 1	Week 2	Week 3	Week 4
Income	$15	$15	$15	$15
Expenses	treats: $3 bags: $5	$0	treats: $3	$0
Profit	$7	$15	$12	$15
Savings Running Total	$7	$22	$34	$49

Track Your Money

It's important to keep track of your money. It is a good idea to write down your income, expenses, and savings. This will help you to stay on track with your savings plan. You can make a chart on paper or use a spreadsheet or an app.

Plan, Prepare, and Save

People use money to get the things they need and want. The money is exchanged for goods and services. At times, people want to buy things that do not cost a lot of money. They may want candies or small toys. Other times, they may want to make big purchases, such as concert tickets or video games. Either way, it is best to make a plan for earning, spending, and saving money.

It takes time and energy to plan what to do with your money. But it is worth the effort. The more you plan and take time to create a budget, the easier it will be to stick to your plans and reach your financial goals.

Allowance

Most children don't have jobs. But in the United States, two out of three parents give their children an allowance. This is money that children earn. They can choose to spend it as they wish. Or they can save the money toward a goal.

Date	Check / ATM Transaction Description	✔	Purchases & Withdrawals (-)	Returns & Deposits (+)	Balance
9 7 0 JUN 19 '00		5			190 —
				100 —	290 —
				20 —	310 —
JUN 2 6 2000				20 —	330 —
9 7 0 JAN 4 '02	95	M		100 —	430 —
9 7 0 APR 14 '03		au		100 .	=530 —
9 7 0 AUG 18 '03		8			
9 7 0 JAN 10 '04		MH			
AUG 1 8 2005			45 —		575 —
9 70 3/14/09 llll				15 .	590 —
9 70 4/19/12			250 —		840 —
				25	865 00

Account books help people track their earnings, spending, and savings.

Ask It!

Make a list of local business owners. Set up a time to interview one of these owners about their business. Have an adult go with you to the interview.

Ask the owner about their experiences. You can use these questions or create your own. Then, share what you learn with your friends.

- When and why did you start your business?

- What things do people often forget to do before starting a business?

- If you could start over, what would you do differently? What would you do the same way?

- How have you stuck to your financial goals? In what ways has it been easy? In what ways has it been hard?

- What advice can you give to someone starting a business?

29

Glossary

bank accounts—arrangements in which people store their money at banks

budget—a plan for how an amount of money will be spent or saved

bulk—large amounts

counterfeiting—making an exact copy of something to trick people into thinking it's real

debit cards—cards that can be used to buy things by taking money directly out of bank accounts

expenses—goods or services that need to be paid for

financial—having to do with money

intimidating—something that makes someone afraid or nervous

invest—to spend money in a way that will make you more money

manage—to have control of something

patience—the ability to remain calm when dealing with difficult or upsetting things

sales tax—an amount of money added to the price of goods and services that is paid to the government

value—importance or worth

Index

Your Turn!

It is never too early to start planning for your future. When you choose a career path, it is important to find something that pays well and that you enjoy doing. Think of some career options that seem interesting to you. Research how much each job pays. Also research the requirements for the job. Do you need to go to college? Do you have to get a certificate? Share your findings with an adult.